What Our Readers Have Said...

Applicability

"These books are great tools that should be used as guidelines for our everyday supervisory practices. You need to take the time to do a short self-evaluation when reading them."

•

"The Pinpoint Training Series delivers information that could be used in a lot different areas."

•

"The things and problems we deal with everyday are discussed in these books."

Convenience

"I like this because I can take them with me to read at a convenient time. I feel the little time I have to spend in the office is best use on activities that directly relate to revenue opportunities. I like the short amount of time it takes to keep up with these."

•

"I prefer the self-study approach; it fits in with my schedule."

•

"I like the fact that the format allows the books to be reviewed as time permits. All work has been conducted on personal, evening/weekend time."

•

"Easy to use... if you put the time into it."

Challenge

"My thought is that the real value of these books comes into effect when doing the action plans."

•

"I like the fact that the format allows assignments to be reviewed as time permits."

Clarity

"Short and sweet. These books are easy to comprehend."

•

"Easy to use, understand, and reference if needed."

Relevance

"I have enjoyed reading these books. They are relevant to today's work environment and the ongoing change in the way we manage our workforce."

•

"I believe the contents of the Pinpoint series are excellent. It causes one to reflect on the daily dynamics in working with oneself as well as with management and peers."

A Team's Function, Purpose & Use

Pinpoint Leadership Skill Development Training Series

TIMOTHY F. BEDNARZ

MAJORIUM
BUSINESS PRESS

Pinpoint Leadership Skill Development Training Series
"A Team's Purpose, Function & Use"
Timothy F. Bednarz

Graphic design: Monika Pawlak

Majorium Business Press
2025 Main Street
Stevens Point, WI 54481
715.342.1018 • 800.654.4935

ISBN 978-1-882181-78-0

Printed in the United States of America

Introduction

The Pinpoint Leadership Skill Development Training Series is designed for targeted training and education regarding increased improvement in a specific skill or competency.

Each book within this series is designed to be easy to use, understand and apply to your job. It can be used as a basis for training individuals, as a discussion guide or as a personal training tool.

Each chapter within this book discusses a specific concept. When you have completed all eight chapters you should have a 360° perspective of the topic.

Additionally, each chapter is divided into specific sections:

- The first section provides you with an overview of the topic
- The Implications section discusses why the concept is important, and why it is important to learn and apply.
- The Strategies, Tips & Techniques to Apply section teaches how to use and apply the particular concept to your work.
- The Points to Ponder section gives you something to think about or to be discussed with a group setting. These are questions not meant to be immediately answered, but to be pondered over time.
- The Training Activity section provides you with the tools to transfer what you have learned to your job. It is designed to help create an action plan to effectively apply the concept.

Each of the topics in this series is time-tested and proven in the marketplace. They have been used by thousands of employees as training tools. Many of the users have commented that what made these books valuable, was the ability to refer to them when a problem surfaced. They indicated that they remembered reading about the exact problem. They referred back to these books and found an appropriate solution.

You will find them equally valuable as a resource in your professional development library.

Table of Contents

LEARNING OBJECTIVES:

- To identify the elements and factors constituting an effective team.
- To identify the critical factors and benefits of teams and the impact they have upon an organization.
- To understand the implications and ramifications that either enhance, or diminish a team's function and process.
- How to overcome the problems and pitfalls associated with team structuring.
- How to apply effective strategies to enhance team functions and purposes.
- How team structuring and its purpose impacts the decisions it makes.

1

Teams Are Carefully Designed

Teams are a critical component of every organization as the predominant vehicle for decision making and accomplishing tasks. A team is defined as a group of people who need each other to accomplish specific results.

Teamwork represents a set of values that encourages listening, responds constructively to views expressed by others, gives others the benefit of the doubt, provides support and recognizes the interests and achievements of others. These values help teams, their individual members, and the entire organization perform.

IMPLICATIONS – WHAT THIS MEANS TO YOU

In many organizational environments, working groups and teams are both essentially used in the same way despite there being a measurable difference between the two. Working groups are simply a loose combination of individuals working toward a common goal. These groups' structures will vary according to the makeup and personalities of the members. Teams, on the other hand, are governed by a specific structure that takes into account member roles, responsibilities, rules and boundaries.

It is important for leaders to understand the distinctions between groups and teams. Most individuals who work within groups perform as individuals. Teams require a common commitment to which members hold themselves mutually accountable. They are committed to a common purpose and a set of performance goals and approaches.

STRATEGIES, TIPS & TECHNIQUES TO APPLY

Teams differ fundamentally from working groups because they require both individual and mutual accountability. Teams go beyond group discussion, debate and decision making and do more than simply share information and best practice performance standards.

To understand how teams deliver extra performance, it is important for leaders to distinguish between teams and other forms of working groups.

Results and Accountability

A key distinction between groups and teams is found in performance results. A group's performance is a function of what its individual members do as individuals: members don't take responsibility for results other than their own, nor do they attempt to develop incremental performance contributions requiring the combined work of two or more members.

A team's performance includes both individual results and the collective results of the team. The collective results reflect the joint and real contributions of team members.

Leadership

A strong and clearly focused leader typically directs working groups. Due to the nature of the group's leadership, the individual leader has the ability to influence the work and results the group produces.

Teams, on the other hand, develop shared leadership roles that are established by team members. This reduces the influence of a single team member on the results of the team.

Purpose

Working groups focus on a purpose that is the same as the broader organizational mission, whereas teams focus on a specific team purpose for which they are established to address.

Output

Teams produce discrete work products through the joint contributions of their members. Possible performance levels are greater than the sum of the individual contributions of its members. Working group performance, however, is simply the product of the results of individual members.

Meetings

Working groups perform their work in efficiently run meetings. Teams encourage open-ended discussions and active problem solving throughout their meetings. The team meeting is specifically structured to encourage these activities. Within this structure, meetings are guided and directed by the roles and responsibilities of team members and are defined by the boundaries and framework established by the team to govern its activities.

Measurement

Working groups measure their effectiveness indirectly by their influence on others. Teams measure performance by directly assessing the collective results of the team and its ability to fulfill its purpose and mission. The results of the team make something specific happen, and that adds real value to the results. By contrast, gathering as a working group from time to time does not sustain the group's performance.

Methodology

Working groups discuss, decide and delegate the work of the group to individual members or committees. Teams discuss, decide and then complete the real work required together as a team. Within teams, performance goals are compelling; they challenge individuals to commit themselves as a team to make a difference within the organization. Since goals are challenging, the onus is on the team alone to make it happen.

POINTS TO PONDER – SOMETHING TO THINK ABOUT

1. How aware of the difference between working groups and teams were you?
2. Do you see how a true team approach in your workplace may be effective?

TRAINING ACTIVITY – APPLICATION & ACTION PLAN

1. Identify the groups/teams that you are involved with at work.
2. Evaluate each according to the following attributes to determine if it is a working group or team, regardless of how it is labeled.
    - Leadership
    - Purpose
    - Output
    - Meetings
    - Measurement
    - Methodology

2

Teams Serve an Organizational Purpose

The formation of teams creates substantial and sustainable long-term benefits for the organization, including the fostering of a self-managing environment where employees are fully empowered to make decisions that increase their efficiency, effectiveness and overall productivity.

IMPLICATIONS – WHAT THIS MEANS TO YOU

Many organizations will transition from groups and committees to formally structured teams with specific goals and objectives that are chartered by the organization to fulfill a specific purpose. Within the company, the transition can be either smooth from one environment to another, or sudden, resulting in traumatic organizational changes.

It is important for leaders to understand that the nature of a team is based upon a discipline that the team structure imposes on itself. Teams create a fully empowered environment that allows organizations to become more efficient, effective and productive. This shift provides companies with the flexibility to become more adaptive to the forces of change, and as a result the world has witnessed an overall increase in global competition in virtually every industry.

STRATEGIES, TIPS & TECHNIQUES TO APPLY

Many organizations purport to have so-called team environments, but some standard working groups are mislabeled or misidentified as teams. Some of the most common groups to be mislabeled as teams are discussed below.

Committees

Organizational committees usually serve as an investigative or advisory body reporting to an appointed person or to the one who organized them.

Task Forces

Organizational task forces are temporary problem solving groups formed to deal with issues that overlap lines of authority. A task force may, for its duration, be full or part time.

Quality Circles

Quality circles consist of groups of employees and supervisors who are seeking ways to increase the effectiveness of workgroups through higher productivity and improved quality.

Project Groups

Project groups are organized to work specifically on a project such as a new product or a new facility. Like the task force, the project group may have a temporary existence. When its mission is accomplished, the group disbands.

Teams have many traits that distinguish them from groups. They are normally chartered to fulfill a specific organizational purpose. The most distinguishing characteristic of a team is that its members have as their highest priority the accomplishment of team goals. The most important business at hand is the success of the team in reaching the collective goals set by its members. Members support one another, collaborate freely and communicate openly and clearly with one another. Effective teams are able to accomplish their organizational purpose within specific areas, as outlined below.

Information

Within the effective team environment, information flows freely—horizontally, vertically and to the entire team. There is a full sharing of information among team members, and individuals are open and honest about what they are communicating with each other.

Personal Relationships

As the team environment develops and is fostered, nurtured and sustained, relationships on the team become more trusting, respectful, collaborative and supportive. Individuals learn to work together and respect one another's input, perspective and opinions.

Conflict

Within a healthy team environment, conflict is regarded as natural and helpful when it centers around examining issues and key points that need to be addressed and is confined to issues, not personalities. In most group environments conflict is often rooted in personal traits, motives and agendas that tend to be destructive to everyone involved. Once the team environment is fostered and developed, most team members will use conflict constructively to address issues, solve problems and make decisions by examining all aspects of each element.

Team Atmosphere

As team members learn to work with each other in an effective team environment, they become more trusting, respectful, collaborative and supportive, creating an open and nonthreatening environment in which to operate.

Decisions

Decisions in the team environment are arrived at by consensus rather than by a majority vote or by forcing members to agree with the decision of the group. By arriving at a consensus, each team member is fully committed to a full and efficient use of the resources available to the team. In this manner each team member is fully responsible for the decision of the entire team.

Creativity

Within many organizational groups, the emphasis is on activity and end input, rather than output and solutions. Within an effective team environment, the team members create more solution-oriented outcomes. The focus of the group is on results, not activity.

Power Base

Within many organizational groups, it is not uncommon to see power hoarded by individuals or small groups based on internal politics and personal agendas. However, in an effective team environment the power of the team is shared by all of its members. It is based on the competence of each member and the contributions that each makes to the team.

Motivation

Within many organizational environments individual achievement is valued without concern for the group. Individuals and groups place their personal interests over and above the interests of the organization. However, on a team, the individual members set the environment for a commitment to group goals. Rather than being coerced and pressured to go along with imposed goals, members find that there is more chance for achievement through the advancement of the team.

Reward

Within many organizational groups the basis for rewards is often unclear. They can be based on subjective and often arbitrary appraisals of performance, favoring specific individuals over others. However, within an effective team environment the rewards are based on the contribution that the group provides to the organization. The team, rather than individuals within the team, is rewarded for its performance.

POINTS TO PONDER – SOMETHING TO THINK ABOUT

1. Have you believed that working within groups and committees is a team activity?
2. What benefits do you perceive in imposing a team discipline upon a working group or committee?

TRAINING ACTIVITY – APPLICATION & ACTION PLAN

1. On a sheet of paper, list the following nine characteristics:
    - Information
    - Personal Relationships
    - Conflict
    - Team Atmosphere
    - Decisions
    - Creativity
    - Power Base
    - Motivation
    - Rewards
2. Identify a committee, working group or quality circle that you are currently involved with, and define the group characteristics using the list above.
3. Using the nine characteristics, identify the strengths and weaknesses of the group.
4. Determine how the discipline of the team structure might improve each of these characteristics.

3

Developing a Team Focus

A group does not become a team until it can hold itself accountable as a team. This requires discipline that brings the team together with a common purpose, approach and responsibility. This discipline is critical to the success of all teams. Yet, effective teams also have a focus within the organization.

IMPLICATIONS – WHAT THIS MEANS TO YOU

Trust and commitment are the results of individuals working toward a common objective. Consequently, teams enjoy a strong common purpose and approach that holds them responsible both as individuals and as a team for their performance. This sense of mutual accountability produces the rich reward of equal achievement that is shared by all team members.

This topic is of critical importance to leaders because teams are becoming the primary unit of performance management in many organizations. This does not mean that teams will crowd out individual opportunities in a formal hierarchy: teams will enhance existing structures without replacing them. Team opportunities exist anywhere hierarchy and organizational boundaries inhibit the skills and perspective needed for optimal results. Teams have a unique potential to deliver results to the organization in these situations.

Organizations must create the kind of environment that enables performance by teams, individuals and the organization.

Groups established as teams with the primary purposes of job enhancement, communication, organizational effectiveness or excellence rarely become effective. Only when appropriate performance goals are set can the process of discussing objectives and approaches give team members clear alternatives. At that point they can disagree with the goal and the path that the team selects; in effect, they can opt out, or they can pitch in and become accountable with and to their team members.

Most effective teams are classified in one of three ways.

Teams That Recommend

These teams include task forces, project groups, audit groups, quality groups and safety groups that are asked to study and resolve particular problems. Teams formed to render recommendations almost always have predetermined completion dates. Two critical issues unique to such teams are getting off to a fast, constructive start and dealing with the ultimate handoff required to get their recommendations implemented.

The key to the issue of a fast start lies with the clarity of the team's charter and the composition of its membership. In addition to wanting to know why and how their efforts are important, task forces need a clear direction as to time commitment and the people senior management expects to participate. Management can assist these groups by ensuring the inclusion of individuals with the skills and influence necessary for crafting practical recommendations that will carry weight throughout the organization.

The ultimate handoff is almost always a difficulty for such teams. To avoid this, teams should transfer the responsibility for recommendations to those who must implement them. The more that senior management assumes recommendations will just "happen," the less likely this will be the case. The more involvement team members have in executing their recommendations, the more likely they will get implemented.

Teams That Make or Do

These teams include people at or near the front lines who are well acquainted with the value-added activities of the organization and responsible for basic manufacturing, development operations, marketing, sales or service. With some notable exceptions, such as new product development or process design teams, these teams tend to have no set completion dates, as their activities are ongoing and continuous.

These teams have the greatest impact on their organization when they focus on the company's critical delivery points. These are the places where the cost and value of products and services are most directly determined. Performance at these points depends upon combining multiple skills, perspectives and judgments in real time. Here the team option is considered the smartest direction for organizations to proceed.

Teams that make or do must have a relentless focus on performance. Senior management must make clear, compelling demands on these teams and pay constant attention to their progress with respect to both team basics and performance results.

Teams That Run Things

Despite the fact that many leaders refer to the group reporting to them as a team, few groups accept this label. Groups that become real teams seldom think of themselves as a team due to the high degree to which they are focused on performance results.

The main issue these teams face is the determination of whether a real team approach is appropriate to the situation. As many entities can be more effective as working groups than teams, the key is to decide whether individual performances will suffice or substantial and incremental performance through real team products is required.

Working groups present fewer risks in that they need little time to shape their purpose since the leader usually establishes it, meetings are run regardless of prior ties to agendas, and group decisions are implemented in relation to specific individual assignments and accountabilities.

In practical terms, most teams that run things tend to be smaller, 2-4 people.

POINTS TO PONDER — SOMETHING TO THINK ABOUT

1. Have you been involved in organizational groups and teams, such as quality circles, that have been abandoned by your company due to a failure to meet specific goals?
2. What has been the experience with team development in your organization over the past several years?

TRAINING ACTIVITY — APPLICATION & ACTION PLAN

1. Identify two or three working groups or teams that you have been involved in. Listed below are several focal points that many teams are involved with.
    - Job Enhancement
    - Communication
    - Organizational Effectiveness
    - Excellence
    - Teams That Recommend
    - Teams That Make or Do
    - Teams That Run Things
2. Select the primary focuses of the groups that you have been involved with in the past.
3. Identify any additional focuses of the group or team you were involved in.
4. In retrospect, note what the appropriate focus of the group should have been.
5. Determine the differences between the actual focus and the optimal focus.

4

There Is No Such Thing as Creating a Trouble-Free Team

Problems can arise throughout team development and management, but leaders must pay particular attention to the structure and focus of the team. There are many potential pitfalls associated with establishing a team's mission and focus. These foundational problems can linger and hinder the team's performance.

IMPLICATIONS — WHAT THIS MEANS TO YOU

Teams can encounter many problem areas during their tenure, but most challenges arise during the establishment of the team. Without a strong foundation that includes a focus, a mission, rules, boundaries and objectives, teams will encounter chronic problems.

It is important for leaders to understand that team productivity will be diminished without a firm foundation. From the outset leaders must invest time and effort in team development to ensure long-term success. This process includes establishing a clear understanding of what to avoid in order to prevent future problems.

STRATEGIES, TIPS & TECHNIQUES TO APPLY

Quality improvement is a common task given to teams. Organizations with teams in this area often stumble into pitfalls and produce poor outcomes. The selection of the wrong process for a team to work on is the main cause of inappropriately focused teams.

Selection of a Project No One Is Interested in

As organizations assign and develop teams for various projects, one common problem stems from selecting projects neither managers nor team members are concerned about. Consequently, the project will likely die from inattention. Often individual team members are assigned to several teams, and will only focus their attention on the projects they are interested in.

Often the only motive that sustains the effort of the team is the commitment of its members. If uninterested in a project, individuals will resist it, hampering the team's ability to meet and work together effectively. When leaders develop new teams, the projects they assign should be meaningful to the active team members.

Selecting a Desired Solution

Leaders tend to think they already know which improvements need to be made before a team meets to study a problem, analyze it and make recommendations. Consequently, they pick a solution for the team to consider rather than have it look at the larger quality improvement process. This tendency does not empower teams to come up with changes and improvements, and their creativity is held back. As a result, the most creative and effective solutions may not be brainstormed, recommended, analyzed, studied and considered, and the team's effectiveness and productivity are diminished.

While the leader's predetermined changes may in fact turn out to be the best way to proceed, teams should be allowed to arrive at their own conclusions, and be free to recommend actions they determine will yield the greatest success.

Projects in Transition

As companies evolve, many processes and projects are in transition. It is wasteful to assign a team a project or process that is undergoing transition or is scheduled for change. The exception here is if changes occur in a process because of the team. In such a case, the team's resources can be effectively used to study and evaluate the process and determine the best changes.

Selecting a System

Managers often delegate projects that are too ambitious and that should be broken down into smaller components. Properly focusing teams on particular elements of a project facilitates a better chance of success. In this manner they can concentrate their efforts and make recommendations that are easily implemented. Once improvements are made in one small area, teams can methodically move on to other areas. This method allows them to build on their successes and, ultimately, to impact the entire system.

Improper Framing of the Problem

When problems are properly framed, team operational boundaries are defined. But teams can frame a problem too narrowly or broadly.

Broadly defined problems can create projects that are too vague or difficult to label. Consequently, teams quickly find they have neither the time nor resources to deal with such projects. Potential solutions also become broadly defined, ineffective and difficult to implement.

Narrowly defined problems create ineffective solutions. Tight parameters prevent teams from exploring all aspects of the problem and its possible solutions. The final solution can result in issues and concerns that are ignored but should have been considered.

POINTS TO PONDER — SOMETHING TO THINK ABOUT

1. How do you feel teams can effectively be employed in your organization?
2. Do you feel that teams in your organization are adequately focused?

TRAINING ACTIVITY – APPLICATION & ACTION PLAN

1. Identify three or four working teams that you are familiar with.
2. Analyze the use of these teams in your organization and determine if they have been effective.
3. Identify any problems or pitfalls you see these teams experiencing.
4. Based on your analysis, how can these teams improve their performance and effectiveness?

5

A Team's Function Is Only as Good as the Strategies Employed

Leaders must learn how to help their teams achieve incremental success. When teams are created, leaders must prioritize their work projects, as an overly ambitious plan can easily destroy a new and inexperienced team.

IMPLICATIONS – WHAT THIS MEANS TO YOU

During initial team formation and empowerment, leaders and employees can feel motivated, eager to start the process. But leaders should exercise caution at this point by maintaining a systematic approach to team formation and project selection. Without sound strategies to develop team foundations and projects, leaders can easily find themselves managing teams that are floundering or failing.

It is better for leaders to carefully build teams with a firm foundation and appropriate projects than to rush into the process and fail. For many teams, small successes that yield immediate, tangible results can be more productive than a far off, major success. Leaders will find that interlinked objectives building upon one another can produce greater results over time than one large and perhaps overly-ambitious project. In this manner, progress is easily measured while also motivating and building team confidence. As teams develop, this process will aid in their maturation and prepare them to tackle more demanding and complex projects.

STRATEGIES, TIPS & TECHNIQUES TO APPLY

Leaders must understand that it takes time to properly create and develop teams. When team building is effectively done, benefits are realized in improved processes, greater productivity, high worker morale and increased customer satisfaction.

As leaders empower teams to facilitate change in the workplace, it is imperative to give them projects with a high probability of success until the team is fully integrated into the organization. Leaders must understand that much is at stake when teams are initially employed because the organization focuses special attention on the project's success or failure.

The following guidelines will aid leaders in selecting initial projects for teams. Additionally, these same criteria can be modified for projects and team development well into the transformation of the organization.

Process

When teams are first developed, there is a natural tendency for leaders and members to become overly ambitious in their goals and objectives. Until the team has matured to the point where members are working well together, it is recommended that leaders encourage the undertaking of tightly focused and easily accomplished projects. The following are selection criteria for team projects:

- The results should have a direct impact on the company's customers.
- The process should recycle approximately once a day. As a result, the changes recommended and implemented by teams will likely become evident within a few weeks. With frequent cycles, teams are able to quickly evaluate the effect of their decisions, study the impact and make necessary process changes.
- Selected processes should not be subject to any other major transition or be evaluated by any other team using methods in application. However, if the purpose of the process is to study how to make transitions, then this guideline does not apply.
- Teams should start with relatively simple processes with clearly de-

fined start and end points. If teams would rather start with a large or complex system, then leaders should encourage breaking it down into smaller components.

- A substantial group of leaders should agree that the process selected is important to the company and its customers.

Area

There are a couple criteria to consider when deciding upon the area in the organization that teams can have the most impact:

- The area selected should allow leaders, supervisors and operators the opportunity to cooperate and fully integrate themselves with teams. This criterion ensures the utmost input, feedback and accountability from all concerned.
- Especially important during the initial stages of team projects, the area selected should be highly visible. This decision ensures that subsequent team results will be visible to the entire organization.

Projects

Leaders need to balance projects within their team environment. Criteria include:

- Leaders should determine that at least half of the projects they select have the potential to produce significant and measurable financial savings for the organization.
- They should ensure that at least half of the projects involve individuals who are relatively low in the organizational hierarchy.
- At least one of their projects should involve interdepartmental collaboration.

As leaders identify potential projects, the application of these criteria would help filter out those ideas least likely to succeed and thus focus teams on the best project candidates. By keeping teams focused and projects well-defined, leaders ensure that they have the greatest opportunity for success.

Leaders can ensure that projects succeed with small, easily obtainable steps. The process should be entered into slowly and deliberately, allowing the team to mature. Leaders who utilize these techniques help foster the desire in team members to tackle increasingly difficult tasks and assignments. The difficulty of the tasks teams take on will correspond to their gains in maturity and experience.

POINTS TO PONDER — SOMETHING TO THINK ABOUT

1. Have you witnessed or experienced situations where teams were formed too quickly and thus highly motivated only in their initial efforts?
2. How have team projects been identified and implemented in the past?

TRAINING ACTIVITY — APPLICATION & ACTION PLAN

1. Select two or three project areas that you think could be effectively assigned to teams.
2. Verify that the project is related to a key organizational issue.
3. Determine if the process targeted for improvement has a direct impact on the organization's customers.
4. Identify if leaders throughout the organization agree that it is an important issue to study and improve.
5. Ascertain whether a sufficient number of managers, supervisors and employees will cooperate to make the project successful.
6. Decide if the project or process is well-defined with clear starting and ending points.
7. Based upon your evaluation, identify and prioritize the projects that are closely aligned with the criteria discussed in this lesson.

6

Why Teams Fail

Teams can fail for a number of reasons. Unspoken issues, personal agendas, competing loyalties and a lack of structure and direction arc just a few examples. It might take time and investigation for leaders to understand these underlying problems. Leaders should also be aware that most problems require a structured approach and solution.

IMPLICATIONS – WHAT THIS MEANS TO YOU

While teams can be effective at resolving problems, handling projects, and improving work processes, it is not uncommon for their success to be hindered at times. It is the leader's duty to mold a group of individuals into an efficient and productive team. However, in a newly formed team setting people will bring issues, agendas and personalities with them that will not always be automatically overcome. Leaders must bear in mind that time, guidance and direction are needed to provide teams with an opportunity to work together and develop trust and cohesiveness.

It is important for leaders to understand that team dynamics provide members with rules, boundaries and structure. These elements help the team overcome specific personality issues, agendas and unspoken problems. As teams learn to operate in a structured environment, they will overcome any issues that hinder their performance.

STRATEGIES, TIPS & TECHNIQUES TO APPLY

It is not uncommon for teams to experience difficulty when starting and ending a project. Additionally, many will flounder in the middle of a project, wondering what actions to take next.

At the beginning of projects, teams will sometimes encounter "false starts" as well as directionless discussions and activities. As teams attempt to progress, individual members can resist moving from one phase to the next. At the end of a project, teams may unnecessarily postpone decisions because they feel something is missing or unfinished.

When problems emerge at the beginning of a project, it suggests that the team is unclear about or overwhelmed by the dimensions of their assignment. Start-up problems may also indicate that team members are not yet comfortable enough with one another to engage in real discussions and make decisions.

Struggles with the decision making process are a sure sign that the team's work is not the product of a consensus: some members may be reluctant to vocally challenge the team's conclusions.

A number of problems can occur at the end of a project. When teams hesitate after completing a phase, it usually indicates that they lack a clear plan to move the process forward. Hesitation can also stem from team members developing a bond during the project and being reluctant to separate at its end. Finally, team members may be reluctant to expose their work to review and possible criticism.

When leaders see their teams floundering, utilizing specific techniques discussed in this lesson can help refocus the project.

Team Plans

One of the primary causes for floundering is an ineffective or ill-conceived team plan. The first step of the team process should define the team's parameters and boundaries. The plan specifies the steps that need to be taken and implemented, the roles and responsibilities of each member, and the objectives of the team. When teams flounder, it is imperative that leaders review the plan with members to pinpoint problems.

Action

After reviewing the plan, leaders should encourage team members with specific steps to move forward. One cause of team reluctance is a fear of failure. But leaders should encourage individuals to embrace their mistakes since it helps the team learn and grow.

Performance Review

Leaders should work with teams to review what worked or failed. The subsequent insight should shed light on why the team is floundering.

Implementation

After reviewing and evaluating the team's progress, leaders should discuss how to incorporate lessons learned and replicate early successes.

Mission

Leaders should also revisit the team charter and mission. Any ambiguity in the team's mission indicates insufficient guidance and direction for team responsibilities.

Barriers

Teams may be floundering due to hindrances and barriers that prevent progress. Insufficient data, knowledge, and expertise, along with a lack of assurances and support from management can all hinder team performance. The feelings of individual team members can also produce barriers. These hindrances and barriers should be identified, and specific strategies should be employed to overcome them.

Lack of Consensus, or Unfinished Business

Leaders must determine whether there is a lack of consensus to move forward. During meetings, leaders should poll the team to determine if there is unfinished business or issues of contention. These elements should be identified and incorporated into the action plan to move the team forward.

POINTS TO PONDER – SOMETHING TO THINK ABOUT

1. Do your teams move smoothly and effectively from one issue to another, or do they tend to bog down?
2. When working with a floundering team, what was your reaction, and how did you refocus the team?

TRAINING ACTIVITY – APPLICATION & ACTION PLAN

As you create and develop your team, be aware of the following elements:

1. Develop an effective project plan with the team. Ensure that the team's boundaries, parameters, rules and responsibilities are clearly defined.
2. Review the charter and mission with the team to make sure it provides adequate guidance.
3. Identify the resources the team requires.
4. Continually work with the team, and poll individual members to guarantee consensus during each phase.
5. Work with each member to identify unspoken issues, concerns and feelings that have not been addressed.
6. Consistently monitor the progress of the team to guard against it bogging down.

7

Consensus as a Decision-Making Tool

Decisions are made when teams reach consensus, with the goal being to arrive at determinations that best reflect the thinking of the entire team.

IMPLICATIONS – WHAT THIS MEANS TO YOU

Leaders should understand that consensus means finding a solution that is acceptable to and supported by all members. While individuals might not agree with every aspect of the solution or consider it their favored option, when consensus is arrived at no one directly opposes it.

Consensus produces a decision that everyone can live with. To facilitate this kind of agreement, the team must allow each member to fully participate in the decision. As such, the team may take several rounds of discussion to detail all aspects of the decision before a consensus is reached. Leaders should note that while this process is time-consuming and often emotionally draining, it brings team strength. Because consensus requires the input of the entire team, the ultimate decision is much more sound than the mere opinions of one or two individual members.

STRATEGIES, TIPS & TECHNIQUES TO APPLY

Building consensus is a long process. Therefore, certain team members may attempt to shortcut the procedure by compelling their associates to accept their particular perspective. While this tactic may actually expedite the decision, it cannot be classified as consensus. Without the active participation of the entire team, members will fail to acquire valuable skills in communication, conflict resolution and discussion facilitation. Innovative solutions that can be effectively implemented are produced only when team members are open-minded and creative in collaboration.

Leaders should understand that consensus is not a unanimous vote. As mentioned before, a consensus might not represent everyone's first priority: it may require substantial compromise.

Additionally, building consensus is different than conducting a majority vote. With a majority vote only part of the team gets something they are happy with, leaving most others feeling snubbed. Consensus, on the other hand, creates a solution that factors in everyone's point of view. Yet, even though consensus often means everyone is satisfied in some way, rarely is an individual member totally satisfied with the solution.

Leaders need to understand, however, that it would be impossible for every decision to receive the support of all members. Indeed, arriving at consensus on every minor decision can create gridlock. Teams should proactively decide which decisions require consensus. Generally, decisions that have a major impact on the direction or conduct of the team—such as which problems to study or ground rules to establish—should be supported by consensus.

The various methods of arriving at consensus include:

Brainstorming

Brainstorming is used to collect ideas from all participants on the team without criticism or judgment. This technique gives members an easy way to examine a broad range of options and generate a list of ideas for consideration.

Successful brainstorming techniques foster creativity and a free-flow of ideas. As a problem solving model, brainstorming normally generates excitement and encourages member involvement. This process often produces innovative solutions to problems.

Multi-Voting

Multi-voting utilizes a straw poll where members prioritize the solutions created during a brainstorming session. Team members cast a series of votes with each stage decreasing the list by half or more, eventually reducing the list to a group of workable solutions.

Nominal Group Technique

The nominal group technique is a more structured way of generating and narrowing a list of options. This method requires less than the typical amount of team interaction. However, it is an effective tool if all or some members are new to each other, or if the team is working on highly controversial issues and mired in disagreement.

Teams first conduct a formalized brainstorming session to define tasks, introduce and clarify questions, generate ideas and discuss issues. Then a selection of brainstormed options takes place as team members rank the items on cards. All votes are tallied and entered on a Pareto or bar chart.

The option garnering the highest score is presented to the team. If members agree to follow that option, the discussion can end and the team can decide on its next course of action. If members do not agree, the team must further discuss the two or three items receiving the highest scores.

POINTS TO PONDER — SOMETHING TO THINK ABOUT

1. In a team or group environment, have you considered a majority vote to be a consensus?
2. Have you ensured that consensus is actually arrived at on your teams, where all members can support the solution and no member opposes it?

TRAINING ACTIVITY – APPLICATION & ACTION PLAN

1. Identify four or five key decisions that have been made in a group or team setting over the last 30 days.
2. List these on a sheet of paper.
3. Next to each, list your perception of how the decision was made (by consensus or not).
4. Determine whether the decision was made by unanimous vote, majority vote or actual consensus.
5. Compare and contrast your perceptions of the decision making process with how the decision was actually made.

8

If It Looks Like a Team and Acts Like a Team, It Is a Team

A team is a group of individuals with a complex set of relationships. As such, it does not feel, think, have goals or intentions of its own. But team members do possess all of these elements, occasionally sharing similar feelings, and usually sharing a common goal. Therefore, teams must have systems of operations and norms of behavior.

IMPLICATIONS – WHAT THIS MEANS TO YOU

Team identity is defined by how individuals perceive themselves as a team. These perceptions contribute to team cohesion: if members see that their team is different than any other they've ever been a part of, they gain a greater appreciation of their personal differences. A unique team environment will facilitate a vital expression of conflicting opinions—a process that no team can survive without. Consequently, team members will be made aware of the multiple realities that exist on their team that open up the possibility of discovering and achieving more than anyone originally anticipated.

Though teams, as a collection of members, are subject to a number of variables, they derive their strength from overcoming any initial individual differences. Shallow and unproductive team member relationships are avoided when team members focus on their personal needs and carefully consider their own preconceived notions of what a team should be. Without overcoming these inherent differences, the team is limited in discovering its full potential and identity.

STRATEGIES, TIPS & TECHNIQUES TO APPLY

There are several elements and characteristics that define a team. These include:

Synergy

One of the key characteristics of a team is its ability to produce ideas that a single team member could not have thought of on his or her own or at least would not have as quickly. Indeed, a team has the ability to solve complex problems that even the most technically gifted members are often unable to unravel alone. This process stems from a synergy as team members increase their willingness to listen and build on each others' ideas. The experience of new ideas surging from this process initiates the team's unique identity.

Vision

The team's vision and goals contribute to its purpose and objectives. Once established, vision is closely aligned with the team's identity.

Norms

Norms are the unstated rules and patterns of behavior that determine that which is acceptable or unacceptable in almost every team situation. Some norms will concern group behaviors; others will cover individual functions on the team. As teams are created, a discussion of norms is needed in respect to meetings, attendance, roles, decision making, time issues, the larger team process, feedback, questioning, and listening and speaking rules.

Leadership

The leader's role is to help clarify the team's purpose and guide the discussion that establishes specific goals. Leaders also act as guardians of the team's vision. However, they must avoid the pitfall of molding the vision to a preconceived form. Team leaders create an atmosphere that supports and encourages the creativity of each team member.

Qualities and Skills

The team's identity is formed by its norms, leadership style and the skills of its team members. Each member brings a variety of qualities to the team—some obvious and utilizable, others hidden and unrealized. The leader can bring out these buried potentials to benefit the team. As teams evolve and develop, new qualities are required and often discovered where least expected.

Membership

Members are normally selected to be part of a team because they have technical skills related to the particular problem at hand, and may also have a working knowledge of problem-solving and decision-making processes. It is the responsibility of the leader to ensure that their team is comprised of individuals with a wide range of qualities. Leaders will find their teams limited if they select people based on personality, apparent qualities, compatibility or a certain mix of interpersonal skills.

Boundary

The team boundary is the line that separates a team from a working group. Boundaries are most obviously defined by team membership and leadership as well as by its purpose, vision, norms and identity.

Boundaries enable the team to make an impact on outside entities and clarify the actions it ought to perform.

POINTS TO PONDER — SOMETHING TO THINK ABOUT

1. As team leader, how well do you protect your team's vision from being molded into a form that might satisfy one or more members' personal agendas?
2. Do you see adversarial events such as deadlines and competition intensifying the cohesiveness and spirit of your team?

TRAINING ACTIVITY — APPLICATION & ACTION PLAN

1. List your team members' names on a sheet of paper and answer the following:
2. What are the qualifications of each person?
3. Why were they selected to become members of this team?
4. Identify each member's role on the team.
5. Determine if they have a working knowledge in solving problems and making decisions.
6. What are the contributions that each person delivers to the team?

About the Author

Timothy F. Bednarz, Ph.D. is CEO of the American Management Development Group, Inc. For over 20 years he has researched, designed and authored hundreds of learning and development programs used by Fortune 1000 companies.

He is also the author of *Great! What Makes Leaders Great. What They Did, How They Did It and What You Can Learn from It* (2011).

Speaking Availability

Timothy F. Bednarz, Ph.D. is available for speaking engagements for your next meeting or association event. He can be contacted at 800-654-4935 or by e-mail at timothy.bednarz@majorium.com.

Bulk Sales

Bulk sales of this book or any other titles available from Majorium Business Press. Inquiries can be directed to sales@majorium.com, or by phone at 800-6654-4935.

Quick Order Form

Fax orders: 715-342-1118. Send this form.

Telephone orders: Call 800-654-4935 toll-free. Have your credit card ready.

Email orders: sales@majorium.com

Postal orders: Majorium Business Press, 2025 Main Street, Stevens Point, WI 54481, USA.

Please send the following books:

____

____

____

____

Please send more FREE information on:

❑Catalog ❑Speaking/Seminars ❑Mailing Lists ❑Consulting

Name: ____________________________________

Address: __________________________________

City: __________________ State: _____ Zip: _________

Telephone: ________________________________

Email address: ______________________________

Sales tax: Please add 5.5% for products shipped to Wisconsin addresses.

Shipping by air:

United States: $4.00 for first book and $2.00 for each additional product.

International: $9.00 for first book; $5.00 for each additional product (estimate).

Made in United States
Cleveland, OH
05 November 2026

47664329R00026